10-Minute Decorating

10-Minute Decorating

176 Fabulous Shortcuts with Style

Susan Ure

Main Street
A division of Sterling Publishing Co., Inc.
New York

Chapelle Ltd.

Owner: Jo Packham

Editor: Linda Orton

Staff: Areta Bingham, Kass Burchett, Marilyn Goff, Holly Hollingsworth, Susan Jorgensen, Kimberly Maw, Barbara Milburn, Karmen Quinney, Leslie Ridenour, Cindy Stoeckl, Gina Swapp, Sara Toliver, Kim Taylor, Kristi Torsak

Photography: Kevin Dilley, for Hazen Imaging, Inc.
Phil Cordova, Cordova Photography
Luciana Pampalone, Luciana Pampalone Studio
Scot Zimmerman for Scot Zimmerman Photography
Joe Coca, Joe Coca Photography

Library of Congress Cataloging-in-Publication

Ure, Susan
10-minute decorating / Susan Ure.
p. cm.
"A Sterling/Chapelle book."
Includes index.
ISBN 0-8069-7483-4 Hardcover
ISBN 1-4027-0067-9 Paperback
1. Interior decoration. I. Title: Ten minute decorating. II. Title

NK2115 .U73 2001
747--dc21   2001020113

10 9 8 7 6 5 4 3

A Sterling/Chapelle Book

First paperback edition published in 2002
by Sterling Publishing Co., Inc.
387 Park Avenue South, New York, NY 10016
© 2001 by Chapelle Ltd.
Distributed in Canada by Sterling Publishing
℅ Canadian Manda Group, One Atlantic Avenue, Suite 105
Toronto, Ontario, Canada M6K 3E7
Distributed in Australia by Capricorn Link (Australia) Pty Ltd.
P.O. Box 704, Windsor, NSW 2756, Australia
Printed in China
All Rights Reserved

Main Street · ISBN 1-4027-1164-6

Every effort has been made to ensure that all of the information in this book is accurate.

If you have any questions or comments, please contact:

Chapelle Ltd., Inc.
P.O. Box 9252
Ogden, UT 84409

Phone: (801) 621-2777
FAX: (801) 621-2788
e-mail: chapelle@chapelleltd.com
website: www.chapelleltd.com

Susan Ure was born in Washington state, but has spent the last 30 years as a resident of Salt Lake City, Utah. Her formal training was as a counselor in drug and alcohol rehabilitation. However, in the early nineties her instincts and talents led her to establishing and becoming the proprietress of FLORIBUNDA, a most magical and discerning gift shop in Salt Lake City.

As a young girl, Susan's interests were in rearranging her home. Family members would return from work to find the dining room in the living room, and Susan moving all that was "moveable" from one place to another. Her overall talent for decorating, and more specifically in selecting the perfect piece for any spot and window displays, has inspired family, friends, and customers most of her adult life. Susan has three sons, six grandchildren, and lives with her husband and two dogs in the foothills of the Rocky Mountains.

Dedicated to the memory of my mother
LaRae Strom

Table of Contents

Introduction

With the rush and responsibilities of everyday life, there is rarely enough time or money to redecorate as often as desired. *10-Minute Decorating* shares ideas for decorating, oftentimes with items already on hand. A scarf can be knotted and placed around a free-standing mirror, or a simple floral arrangement may be placed on a china shelf containing a collection of unmatched crystal glassware. Whether one is displaying a collection or a few favored objects, simple rearrangments can be done in a 10-minute or less time frame.

Comprehensive design tips on how to add accents are included for virtually every room in the house. A surplus of ideas for lighting, walls, windows, containers, and much more are shown in full-color photographs. Candles can be mixed and matched, unique fabrics may become table covers, and books stacked artfully allow favorite pieces to be displayed at the last moment before guests arrive. Whatever the decorating style may be—country, "shabby chic," Victorian, or contemporary— ideas can be found for 10-minute decorating.

1

Chapter 1
Containers

Containers come in such extraordinary styles and materials. Goblets, jars, bowls, and baskets can be filled with contrasting wonders, limited only by the imagination. No matter what the container, it may hold an equally large content variety.

design idea 1
10-minute tip: Fill a vase with feathers in place of flowers.

This bouquet is made up of peacock, ostridge, and pheasant feathers which in turn complement the antique peacock shawl on the wall.

design idea 2
10-minute tip: Tie a tassel to the lid of a decorative jar.

The clear apothecary jar was filled with seashells and allows one to see the many forms within it much better than if they were sitting in a bowl.

design idea 3
10-minute tip: Fill a treasured container with unexpected contents.

This little cement angel came bearing gifts. In the bowl, she holds colored pieces of glass etched with loving thoughts of peace, hope, and joy. An embossed velvet scarf is casually placed about her neck. When she is placed in the bathroom, her bowl may contain bars of soap.

2

3

4

5

design idea 6
10-minute tip: Vases can be made from various objects.

Bring a garden element indoors by stacking two clay flowerpots, with bottoms together, and securing them together with glue. Place a glass filled with water inside the top flowerpot to hold fresh flowers, and tie a pretty ribbon bow to hide the glued edges.

design idea 4
10-minute tip: The simplicity of a single vase or object on a shelf or countertop can produce a dramatic impact.

This urn-style vase and the arrangement of the parrot tulips add contrast to the background color of a painted wall.

design idea 5
10-minute tip: Use repetition or multiples of a design element when decorating a room or tabletop.

The brick wall is the backdrop for three clear glass vases that reveal lime, orange, and lemon slices. Fresh florals were added to an inner container with the fruit slices placed in the outer vase. Both the inner and outer containers are filled with water. Shells, nuts, seeds, and twigs—without the water—could be substituted for the fruit slices.

6

design idea 7
10-minute tip: Vary the sizes and heights of vases and arrangements.

Several vases are placed along the stair—an unexpected place for displaying flower arrangments. An assortment of colorful roses and lilies add an element of interest to the large white wall behind them, and the scent of the flowers is an added bonus.

design idea 8
10-minute tip: Place transparent vases in front of a window to enable the natural light to shine through.

The leaded glass has a Frank Lloyd Wright style of design and the cobalt blue containers repeat it. The straight lines of the vases almost become a part of the window. The large white lillies mellow the overall geometric scheme.

design idea 9
10-minute tip: Fill an unused goldfish bowl with a colorful assortment of glass ornament balls.

Make the arrangement more festive by removing the metal top from some of the ornaments and filling them with water. Insert one or more sprays of orchids into the ornaments. One white magnolia was placed into a florist vial, purchased from a floral shop, and nestled in between the ornaments.

7

8

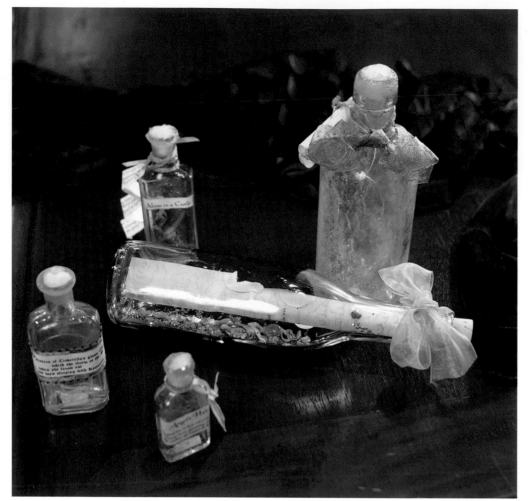

10

design idea 11
10-minute tip: Use colorful sachet bags as decorative elements.

This fluted bowl contains colorful scented sachets tied closed with ribbons. A collection of sewing bobbins, jeweled bracelets, or cherished photos could also be displayed in decorative bowls.

design idea 12
10-minute tip: Look for a new use for old and used items.

An old serving tray, without the glass, and a piece of quilted fabric serve as a surface for the bouquets contained in two crystal and silver goblets that "toast" in Spring.

11

design idea 10
10-minute tip: Recycle old and used bottles with embellishments of ribbons and tags.

Vintage bottles are often appreciated for their antiquity alone. Add a message in a bottle, and one's imagination can go as far as the current of any ocean could carry it. The large bottle lying on its side contains a wedding invitation with sand and shells sent from Hawaii. Create labels and tags either by hand or computer and secure them to bottles.

16

12

Containers as art in their own right are pleasing to the creative spirit. In terms of shape and medium, it is more interesting to create still lifes when placing flowers in vases.

design idea 13
10-minute tip: Look for unique plant cuttings to place in vases. All florals need not stand upright, allow one or more to fall artfully.

The simple composition of this tall and narrow bamboo vase containing onion blossoms creates a tranquil feeling. By changing the arrangement, you can change the entire mood of the setting.

design idea 14
10-minute tip: Use everyday objects when composing artful floral arrangements.

These rice bowls create an artful arrangement. Fresh flowers, inserted into florist vials, are strategically placed into oriental rice bowls filled with dry rice. The composition is completed with chop sticks casually set across the bowl as if ready to be used, or placed vertically in the bowl. This arrangement is very simple, yet elegant. Displays like these may take some planning, but they can be assembled in a matter of minutes.

13

10-minute tip: Do something unexpected such as displaying an eclectic group of items, or placing elements lying down instead of upright.

When a number of items are on display at one time, as on this table, create varying heights to add depth and dimension to the display. The glass vases complement one another, yet are different in shape. The vintage type blocks are arranged lying down rather than standing. Two pieces of fruit are neatly placed in a shallow tray and two carved figures stand side by side, as if guardians of the table. The table arrangement is quite simple, allowing the eye to take in each object. The lightness and variations in shape are subtle and do not distract or add more bulk to a table that already has many items on display.

design idea 16
10-minute tip: Place containers inside of other containers.

A basket within a brass bowl combines smooth and rough surfaces. The woven qualities of the basket are organic, having been made from natural grasses. The design on the metal bowl had its origins in nature, but has a polished metal surface texture. The basket holds an assortment of seashells, extending the rough and smooth qualities of the basket and the bowl. The contrast is quite pleasing from both a visual and a tactile point of reference. The basket is placed on an ethnic-design fabric, then placed in front of framed pieces that lean against the wall.

16

A dearly loved item becomes an **object of desire,** or something you want to have around all the time. In order to accomplish this, try creating a new use for it.

design idea 17
10-minute tip: Use a silver serving tray for flower and candle arrangements

An unusual silver serving dish is filled with an oversized vanilla candle and encircled with ornamental berries and red roses. A florist foam ring was soaked in water and placed on the serving dish. The candle was set inside of the ring, then the stems of the roses were pushed into the foam and secured in place with corsage pins.

design idea 18
10-minute tip: Arrange florals in rows and combine potted plants with cut flowers.

The ceramic basket-weave bowl, whose most common use might be to hold warmed bread, contains assorted roses and miniature violets. The bowl is lined with a clear plastic planter liner, filled with water, and the violets are placed down the center with rows of roses on each side.

design idea 19
10-minute tip: Make a serving tray from plates and glassware.

These parfait and champagne glasses found themselves upside down, placed onto matching plates, and converted into a serving dish. During the holidays, top it off with a candy dish that holds Christmas ornaments and candy.

18

19

design idea 20
10-minute tip: Flowers removed from old hats can be placed in a container.

This handmade ceramic container is filled with silk and velvet flowers and leaves that mimic the clay flower elements along the edge of the container. A pair of pink opera gloves with a matching clasp purse complement the pastels in the dish. A gold metal box from Paris is the final accent to this setting.

20

21

design idea 21
10-minute tip: Use a small branch or vine to make a natural handle for a basket or bowl.

The interior of this small coiled-ceramic basket was filled with berries and freshly picked flowers. A handwoven cloth is the base for this charming scene.

design idea 22
10-minute tip: Place a number of small interesting objects that attract the eye around a main focal point.

A handmade slab vase is the center of attention, but upon closer observation, the details begin to come into play. A tiny ceramic hat is perched on an old alarm clock. A floral-print handkerchief is casually placed on the counter and surrounded by a number of smaller containers.

23

24

design idea 24
10-minute tip: Use edible objects for containers.

Here, the container happens to be a bread bowl and has a hearty visual effect. A container of water was placed inside a hollowed-out bread bowl and filled with berries, grapes, and a single Gerbera daisy.

design idea 25
10-minute tip: Allow a single container to fill an entire space.

A square window embraces a round container that in turn is filled with layers of brightly colored vegetables.

It may be the container that makes the entire statement for an arrangement or the contents that can be seen within it.

design idea 23
10-minute tip: Place fresh fruit or vegetables into a transparent container, fill with water, and place a floating candle on top.

This is a great example of how the contents become the "magic" of this container. A full view of the raffia-bundled carrots reveals the color and freshness of the vegetables.

25

26

design idea 26
10-minute tip: Use edible items and dishes from the kitchen for arrangements and centerpieces.

The large bowl looks like a "Fall" offering to the hostess of a Thanksgiving dinner and the smaller bowl attractively holds fresh bread for the meal. The African violet is potted in its own container and the vegetables are held in place with florist picks.

27

design idea 27
10-minute tip: Use the food that you will be serving as part of the table decorations.

These baskets are filled with colorful fresh peppers and a variety of breadsticks, and their contents are easily accessible when preparing or eating a favorite meal.

design idea 28
10-minute tip: Elegant flowers such as roses can be mixed with fruits and vegetables in floral arrangements.

Roses and lilies are snuggled inside this oriental basket along with miniature pumpkins that set the tone with their rich color.

29

The smooth surface of the measuring cups against the stucco surface of the windowsill is such a pleasing contrast.

design idea 31
10-minute tip: A picture frame can be used for table displays or place settings.

A plain wooden picture frame encloses an artful display of food. What a wonderful surprise it would be to use an assortment of picture frames to "frame" delicious dishes at a dinner party.

30

design idea 29
10-minute tip: Outdoor planters can be brought indoors for uses other than planters.

Handmade clay-chicken planters are sitting pretty with a rustic wooden door and cuttings of raspberry bushes as a backdrop. The natural look of the containers, combined with painted wooden eggs, berries, and fruit scattered around the table, enhances the country theme.

design idea 30
10-minute tip: Display vegetables from the refrigerator or garden in kitchen utensils and containers.

These French ceramic measuring cups are simple, yet artistic in design. The terra-cotta flowerpot of fresh herbs, asparagus, and tomatoes not only adds color, but also ties into the cooking element.

31

32

Chapter 2

Textiles

Fabrics, scarves, quilts, pillows, and laces are some of the most wonderful decorative details in one's home and take but a moment to arrange.

design idea 32
10-minute tip: Make a quick change by placing a throw or delicate fabric across a bed or over a chair.

A velvet throw was placed on the bed and silk fabric was draped over the chair. It is a great way to change a room seasonally or "just because." Layers of fabric add the quality of warmth during fall and winter. In the spring, a layer or two can be removed.

design idea 33
10-minute tip: Bring the throws out of the closet and display them on chairs or other furniture.

This straight-backed chair becomes a resting place for a lovely crocheted throw that softens the look of the chair. The chair and throw create a sense of heritage with the antique desk and old family photographs.

design idea 34
10-minute tip: Fabrics can be layered over tables and knotted.

Fabric was draped over this end table. One piece was twisted and wrapped around the table edge, then knotted to create an elegant look. The table is framed from behind with a live palm.

33

34

35

36

10-minute tip: Bring wearables out of the closet and display them on sofas and chairs.

Surround yourself with beloved items, such as this shawl that was a gift from a wonderful artist. When the shawl is not being worn, it still can be enjoyed when draped across the back of a chaise.

design idea 37
10-minute tip: Use scraps of fabrics for covering pillows that are in need of a change.

A length of fabric covers the back and seat of this overstuffed chair. The neck-roll pillow is covered with a small piece of satin that was a leftover piece from a duvet cover. Each end was tied with satin cording, and no sewing was necessary.

Pillows can be expensive and not something one would want to replace over and over again.

design idea 35
10-minute tip: Change the look of a pillow by wrapping it with a shawl and tying an attractive knot.

When ready for a change, take a piece of fabric—in this case a sari from Bali—and tie or knot it very simply around the pillow. A fringed silk shawl was arranged behind the pillow and a smaller pouch-style pillow was placed in front to add an Oriental element, integrating this look with the remainder of the room.

37

Pillows, pillows, and more pillows—they are terrific to use when needing a quick decoration fix. The fabric of the pillow can say so much.

design idea 38
10-minute tip: Pillows can be placed as decorative elements in places other than on a chair, sofa, or bed.

The hand-painted tulips on this pillow are charming in combination with the lace background, a porcelain figure, and vintage china. The dark color of the pillow is a nice contrast against the white lace of the hutch.

design idea 39
10-minute tip: Mix patterns and textures in pillows to add interest to simple designs.

38

39

The embroidered ribbon edging and fringe on the tube pillow complement the stripes of the fabric-covered chair, as well as the more elegantly patterned and tasseled square pillow.

design idea 40
10-minute tip: Use decorative elements from old clothing and accessories to embellish pillows.

The black crushed-velvet pillow has antique beads attached from a 1920s' flapper dress. This is a much better way to admire the vintage workmanship than keeping it in the attic in a storage box.

design idea 41
10-minute tip: Make a clean and simple statement by placing one attractive pillow on a chair or sofa.

This high-backed wicker chair would seem rigid and uninviting without this single pillow to cushion you. Even if one has to move the pillow to sit back, its presence beckons a guest to have a seat.

design idea 42
10-minute tip: Bring in outdoor furniture and wrap the cushion or twin-sized mattress in fabric.

Simply designed furniture pieces such as this piece of outdoor furniture could appear to be quite cold and stiff without the fabric-wrapped mattress and a selection of pillows loosely tossed across the cushion and along the back.

41

42

Enjoy art in its great variety of forms, and your space will have more history, heritage, and diversity. Not all art hangs on a wall or sits on a table.

design idea 43
10-minute tip: Hang wearables over doors for decorative elements.

These two scarves hung over a door are also wearable art. When they are not being worn, they are used to decorate a door or wall so they can be enjoyed year round.

design idea 44
10-minute tip: Combine various ethnic designs and objects.

The quilt displayed over the wall beam not only draws the eye upwards, but adds an element of art to an otherwise empty space. An unlikley combination is the early American quilt and the Oriental carpet, yet they complement one another and bring continuity and warmth to the room. This room has a minimal amount of accessories such as a single vase on the mantle, but it is this simplicity that allows the quilt and rug to be the primary focus.

44

design idea 45
10-minute tip: Knot the fringe on tablecloths and table runners.

This table runner was placed on top of a hutch and allowed to hang over the edge, displaying the elegant woven pattern. A painted wooden church and metal candlestand with candle make a lovely arrangement and are a quite different approach from a silk floral planter or basket.

design idea 46
10-minute tip: Ribbons and trims can be hung from a rod to make unique wall hangings.

45

46

This ribbon wall hanging accents a corner nook in a more formal setting. A wooden curtain rod is hung on the wall and an assortment of ribbons and trims are cut to graduated lengths and looped over the rod to make a quick and simple wall hanging.

An ivy planter, an old thread spool and wooden cylinders used as candleholders, vintage leather-bound books, and a metal cherub frame containing an old photograph are arranged on the metal filigree and marble end table.

design idea 47
10-minute tip: Drape a vintage scarf and allow it to hang down the side of the surface that it is placed on.

An oversized silk floral arrangement sits on an antique embossed-velvet scarf with beaded fringe. Three decorative bottles complement the arrangement, with a short length of exquisite ribbon knotted around the neck of each bottle.

48

design idea 48
10-minute tip: Make a table runner and napkins from fabric scraps.

A piece of woven yardage picked up on recent travels had the same color scheme that is in the kitchen. The yardage was not wide enough for a tablecloth, so a table runner was the next choice. The fruit-patterned dishes make a lovely yet casual table arrangement. The fresh floral and fruit arrangement on the dinner plate looks good enough to eat, and the coffee mug contains the taller florals while the teacup holds the more delicate and smaller florals.

design idea 49
10-minute tip: Display objects that bring back fond memories.

What a warm welcome when mittens are hung over the fireplace mantle during the winter months. An antique shawl hangs behind the mittens in its usual place. Outgrown and treasured handknitted mittens were strung on a cord then attached to the top of the mantle. They are a gentle reminder of children that were once young and would come running in on cold winter evenings to dry and warm themselves by the fire.

50

51

design idea 50
10-minute tip: Display collections in a hutch or cabinet with glass doors.

Any collectible items such as these quilts, folded neatly behind this vintage glass door, are easy to see and enjoy. It would be a shame to hide them away in a dark cupboard.

design idea 51
10-minute tip: Use a bench or chair for a quilt rack to display quilts.

This bench becomes a plant stand as well as a way to display a beautiful heirloom quilt.

design idea 52
10-minute tip: Use an afghan as a table runner.

This afghan, folded and draped to one side of the trunk, is an example of a quick way to change a color scheme. The copper pots hung on the wall may be more permanent, but the nestled mixing bowls and afghan could be quickly exchanged for other items when desired.

53

design idea 53
10-minute tip: Use a quilt as a shower curtain.

Everything in this bathroom speaks of the past. The quilted shower curtain feels more like an entrance to an event than a simple shower.

Old dresser runners are draped over the toilet tank and held in place by a wooden soda box containing bath toiletries. A decorative bottle contains fresh wildflowers and a battered tin bathtub hangs on the wall. Vintage postcards and greeting cards are randomly adhered above the shower curtain.

design idea 54
10-minute tip: Mix and match colors when hanging towels.

Hand towels trimmed with lace and buttons are placed in this bathroom when guests are expected. Fresh floral sprigs are tied with ribbon and

55

54

hung just above the towels to add fragrance as well as beauty to the room.

design idea 55
10-minute tip: Place a number of doilies in various sizes and styles on a tabletop.

Heirloom doilies crocheted in various patterns adorn a table-top to show off this timeless art. A bowl of dried rosebuds or a clear glass jar make a simple statement and allow the beautiful patterns to be viewed.

56

Lace is a labor of love, and because of the hours of work it takes to create, it becomes a timeless heirloom passed down through generations. Finding unique ways to display such works takes some creativity and a new way to look at decorating.

10-minute tip: Use a tablecloth as a bed canopy.

The scallop-edged lace tablecloth is draped over the four-poster bed. The lace canopy adds an intimate touch. A length of fabric was gathered and attached to one post under the lace, then ballooned. A breakfast table placed on the bed makes this room look ready for the guest.

design idea 57
10-minute tip: Hang a table runner on a mantle or shelf.

When you have a narrow piece of lace, such as this beautifully tasseled lace table runner hung above the fireplace, make it a focal point. It adds warmth and an old-fashioned elegance to this sitting room.

57

Chapter 3

Windows

Simple accents or unconventional use of materials when decorating can change the entire look of a window. Inexpensive materials and a few minutes of labor is all that is often needed.

design idea 58
10-minute tip: Hang a wire shelf across the window and use "S" hooks to hang objects from it.

Teapots and an apron on a coat hanger adorn this fanciful kitchen. Who wouldn't enjoy feasting their eyes on these collected basics? Nothing is wasted here, the retro theme is strong and witty.

design idea 59
10-minute tip: Display favorite dishes in unconventional ways as on this tabletop placed on front of a bay window with a great overlook.

A breakfast nook with a fifties-style metal tabletop is the ideal setting for these vintage dishes and the birdhouse that is hanging inside without obstructing the view of the rose garden.

design idea 60
10-minute tip: Use dish towels for a valance.

This detail of the curtain reveals white dish towels that were converted into a valance displaying the days of the week.

59

60

61

design idea 61
10-minute tip: Draw a curtain up in the middle instead of using tiebacks on the side panels.

Once again, vintage materials have been used to dress up this dining-room window. Antique table lace was draped across the face of the window and pinned in place with push pins. The lace was slightly drawn up in the center and tied with ribbons and dried roses. The striped panels on each side are twin-sized bed covers salvaged from an old cabin. The fabric was gathered at the top, and a large rubber band was looped over the gathered fabric. All the materials for creating this window treatment were right on hand.

The corner window was further accented by a copper bird cage, placed on a small wooden stand, and family photographs, placed off to the side of the curtains on the wall.

design idea 62
10-minute tip: A framed picture can be hung on a door.

The interesting and unconventional look of this window is the use of lace as a backdrop for framed quilt squares. Note the small lace purse hanging from the door hinge—one of those unexpected details.

62

10-minute tip: Add additional decorative elements to
a curtain rod, such as wine bottle decorations.

This detail shows how these wine bottle embellishments, which consist of a cluster of glass grapes with
leaves, were used to add weight as well as a decorative element to this lightweight sequined curtain.
Glass grapes were selected in a hue close to the color
of the curtain. When not serving as a curtain accent,
these same grapes also could be used as napkin rings
or slipped over a doorknob. If something is admired
and one is not certain how to use it, try moving it
around. You will know when you have found the perfect resting place.

10-minute tip: Place sheer curtains over a window
when some privacy is desired without losing the view.

Sheer curtains soften the windows and allow light to
filter in as well as the view of deer on the hillside.
When the window treatment is not the primary focal
point of the window, a subtle fabric may be just the
ticket to accent your decor. The fabric in the curtains
allows the beautiful and rich fabrics such as throws,
coverlets, and pillows, to be the primary focus of this
bedroom.

63

64

65

66

design idea 67
10-minute tip: A necklace or other jewelry can be used to tie back curtains.

A shell necklace pulling back draperies is not only attractive, but unique and visually pleasing. Strings of beads or vintage necklaces would also make unique and lovely tiebacks.

design idea 65
10-minute tip: Slip a plain curtain rod into copper tubing and attach finials for a different look.

This idea came about because copper curtain rods are not available through curtain rod suppliers. Varying panels give this room an eclectic feeling. All of the tabbed panels may be pulled to one side or split wherever desired.

design idea 66
10-minute tip: Drape and wind lengths of sheer yardage over curtain rods.

The manner in which drapes are hung is a fashion statement in itself. The metal curtain rod has flowers and leaves that have been entwined with sheer fabrics, creating a dreamy look.

67

59

69

design idea 68
10-minute tip: Lace scraps can be used as tiebacks for curtains.

A wide piece of scrap lace is used to tie back a drapery panel. Behind the drapery is a lace curtain that brings together the Victorian theme in this room setting.

design idea 69
10-minute tip: Use a table runner as a window valance.

Everything in its place and a place for everything? Not necessarily. This table runner found a new resting place atop a curtain rod. Lace curtains cover the entire window beneath the table runner, and patterned drapes flank each side.

design idea 70
10-minute tip: Layer two curtains over a window and tie one in a knot.

This knotted curtain would look great on a paned-glass door. This look could be repeated with any fabric and contrasting backdrops.

70

design idea 71
10-minute tip: Tie back curtains with tassels.

A single tassel modestly ties back these floral drapes and is simple to slip off when you need to block out the light. A lace valance covers the curtain rod and outer curtain panel to add a softening touch across the window.

design idea 72
10-minute tip: Use kitchen napkins placed over a curtain rod for valances.

Originality keys this setting. A painted door frame covered with lace panels, floral fabric, and white eyelet napkins catches the eye. A set of curtain rods are hung onto the door below the first set of windowpanes and covered with lace panel curtains. Patterned curtains were placed on a second rod above the top windowpanes and pulled back beyond the door frame with tassels. Freshly ironed kitchen napkins top off the look.

73

design idea 74
10-minute tip: Attach a length of fabric to a curtain rod and allow it to swag.

A short wooden curtain rod was attached at one side of the window, rather than across the width of the window. A curtain panel was gathered onto the rod, then a rich fabric with beautiful drape was attached to each end of the rod and allowed to swag below the top of the curtain. This is another variation of how one can play with textiles and try out new and unconventional ways to accent windows.

design idea 73
10-minute tip: Wind a floral garland around a curtain rod.

Valances can be created in a divers number of ways and with a variety of materials. This valance was made by using two lengths of fabric and knotting one end of each length to the curtain rod. Each length was brought to the center of the rod, allowing the fabric to swag. The remaining two ends of the fabric were knotted together to hang from the center of the curtain rod. A garland of silk flowers was then wrapped around the curtain rod and an empty frame was hung over the underlying curtain panels. This window treatment would be used on a window where the draperies are not drawn.

74

64

75

design idea 75
10-minute tip: Attach fabric to a curtain rod with knots.

The curtain is created with two different lengths and types of fabrics, each tied into a knot at one end and swagged over a glass-block window. A particularly interesting effect is the different lengths of the fabric and the fact that the window treatment is also knotted on the hanging end.

design idea 76
10-minute tip: Tie back curtains with oversized tassels.

A layered effect has been applied to this modest window with a window blind behind the curtain when privacy is needed.

76

77

Chapter 4
Walls

Decorating walls is more than applying paint or wall-paper; it is anything that is placed on them or in front of them.

design idea 77
10-minute tip: Hang a shawl or other wearable on the wall in place of framed artwork.

The focal point in this guest room is above the bed where an embroidered silk shawl was hung. Clear push pins were used—rather than a curtain rod—to create the gathered and draped effect with the fringe falling randomly. The fabric falls naturally, as it would if someone was wearing it.

An heirloom piece of lace is draped over the shade on one of the wall-mounted brass lamps. This is an obvious indication of which side of the bed belongs the lady of the house.

design idea 78
10-minute tip: Hang scarves on walls in small spaces.

A silk hand-painted scarf is hung on a narrow wall space next to glass tiles. The small wicker drawers topped with bouquets of ostrich feathers and fresh flowers give a complementary touch to this wall. The feathers repeat the painted motif in the scarf.

78

10-minute tip: Hang original artwork in
the bedroom or less formal areas of the
home where it can be enjoyed by those
who live there.

Original art need not be experienced in
only those rooms where entertaining and
guests may visit. A large blank wall in this
bedroom is just the place for oversized art.
The contemporary style of this room with
its relatively unadorned—except for a
bold-colored paint—walls becomes the
perfect setting for brightly colored original
artwork, whether it is hanging on the wall
or leaning against the wall in a large
alcove at the head of the bed. The alcove
also becomes a bookshelf to hold books
one would like to read or study during
quiet personal times.

79

Picture frames are one way to fill a wall space. How the frames are placed is another matter. Placement can convey formal or informal tones in a room. Balance is a key factor when arranging a group of framed artwork.

design idea 80
10-minute tip: When hanging framed pictures or other objects, try breaking up the pattern with a different shape.

The top of this doorway has a finished look by the way these serving trays are arranged above the doorway. Notice how placing an oval-shaped tray in the middle breaks up the design.

80

design idea 81
10-minute tip: Group four frames of similar size and shape together with a fifth larger picture placed off to the side.

Four smaller frames are placed together and a larger one just to the right creates a nice balance next to a large lamp.

design idea 82
10-minute tip: Place a row of small picture frames underneath larger framed artwork.

81

This is a very nontraditional way to group picture frames on the wall. The lamp helps add balance where another frame might ordinarily be placed.

design idea 83
10-minute tip: Group unusually shaped frames together on a wall.

In this collection, frames are made of similar materials, metal and wood, and contain like subject matter; but that is where the similarities end. This eclectic grouping has an Old Spanish feeling in a room that contains ethnic objects on the table and the doorknob. Although the frames are of very different shapes, the setting has a cohesive feeling.

82

Sometimes one finds a small card or trinket that one simply does not want to live without. Instead of having boxes of these treasures put away, try framing them to display their individuality. Here, two gift cards, which have small pieces of tapestry, beads, and dried lavender, were framed and hung in the bathroom. If one tires of them there, it takes only minutes for them to be relocated somewhere else.

84

design idea 85
10-minute tip: Place colorful oversized prints in small or monochrome settings.

This was a very small and plain bathroom. Everything in the room, including the color, was quiet and subtle. This room needed a spot of bright color or a "color surprise." This oversized print with its bold colors gives the bathroom the dramatic focus and weight that was needed.

Other accessories that brighten and add mood to this monotone bathroom include the orchid and candle sitting on a shelf above the bathtub, along with the elegant shell drawers where another candle sits with assorted shell artifacts.

design idea 86
10-minute tip: Hang decorative objects between shelves.

Sometimes shelves and walls have enough going on. An unexpected place was found for this whimsical clock on the column between the two sets of shelves.

design idea 87
10-minute tip: Place a picture frame on the couch instead of on the wall.

Being unpredictable is the artist's way! An old picture frame that has been in the family for twenty years contained the photograph of a grandmother's friend. The value to the immediate family was not in the photograph, but in the frame. Some dried flowers from the garden were glued onto a piece of mat board and framed.

design idea 88
10-minute tip: Allow a piece of art to fill an entire space, such as from the ceiling to the top of the door jamb.

A narrow space above the doorway in the kitchen needed decoration, and although dishes are often the accessory of choice, something different was desired. This lovely, carved wooden art piece from Mexico was the perfect companion to adorn this particular spot.

87

88

design idea 89
10-minute tip: Glue buttons onto magnets to secure photographs to metal surfaces

Old buttons glued onto magnets enhance the feeling of age, as well as adding color and ornamentation. Other trinkets could be used in place of buttons.

design idea 90
10-minute tip: Hang an old door on the wall and embellish with photographs.

There were too many picture frames hanging on this dining-room wall, and none of the frames were particularly compatible or interesting. Buying new frames for so many pictures would have been much too costly. Found in the garage was an old

screen door that was used in place of the frames. It is a fun way to to display photographs that were previously in frames. To soften the hard edges of the door "frame," a tassel was tossed over one corner of the frame and a piece of old lace was draped over the other. A bouquet of dried roses was attached to the upper edge of the screen. Since the screens were metal, magnets could be used to secure the photographs in place.

89

90

76

Most people see a blank wall and are intimidated with so much open space. No decision must be final when it comes to decorating walls.

design idea 91
10-minute tip: Decorate a wall with individual calendar pages.

An easy solution was applied to this wall by using manila envelopes which have endearing applications of calendar artwork. The random placement of the envelopes around the corner of the desk adds a playful note to the informal artwork in an otherwise more formal setting.

design idea 92
10-minute tip: Place two colorful leaves on the wall for an element that is in itself, beauty and simplicity.

Two autumn maple leaves are placed just above the desk surface. On a larger scale, the simple lines of this open desk accentuate the detail of the faux-painted wall.

An assortment of objects placed on the desk adorn as well as enhance the large wall space behind it. An orchid brings in nature while a sphere on a pedestal and a finial become bookends. A miniature photograph is framed with an extra wide mat and leans against the wall rather informally. Books are arranged in a wire basket as well as stacked on the desk, stool, and floor.

91

93

80

94

design idea 93
10-minute tip: Attach a coatrack to the wall and create an unusual wall grouping.

Everyone needs a place to hang their hat. This conjures up a variety of ways to hang hats, scarves, silk bags, and perhaps even a guardian angel to oversee your comings and goings. A grand hat rack is in good company with assorted keepsakes, offering a sense of luxury. A framed photograph with an embellished mat, a vintage fan, a fabric-framed mirror, and a sign wishing one "Good Night" in French add to the visual feast of this grouping.

design idea 94
10-minute tip: Sponge metallic paint onto wall trim.

Embossed paper was applied to a half-wall in place of traditional wallpaper and border. However, the embossed-paper border needed a little something extra. Metallic acrylic paint from a craft store was sponged onto the border. A complementary piece of ribbon was used to tie back a sheer curtain in lieu of a purchased or more formal tieback. Those small touches, such as paint or a pretty ribbon, make a big difference for little expense and time.

Chapter 5

Minor Details

It is often the minor details that gives a space the creativity and warmth needed to make it more engaging. It is those small additions that is each artist's trademark. View every grouping or item within a room as an expression of art. Whether rearranging a shelf or adding a simple knob or tassel to an armoire, let your personality show through. Most accessories or design details could be used in any room at any time.

design idea 95
10-minute tip: Displays of collections should be changed from time to time to better enjoy each item.

A collection of antique shoes from China and beadwork purses from the 1900s are part of this display.

design idea 96
10-minute tip: Use the flat surfaces of books to display items.

Old reading glasses and other collectible items are artfully placed on and around an antique book for all to see and enjoy.

96

10-minute tip: Tack a scarf onto the corners of a pillow to change the look of a pillow.

When a room's palette is monotone, such as this living room, the minor details create warmth and intimacy. Color is introduced with a few pillows, two of which have had silk scarves tacked onto them. Large plants bring drama and life to the living space. The design of the furniture and the warm tones in the wood grain of the floor need the splash of color in earth tones to complete the look.

The dark antique Japanese wedding chest has detail of its own, but is lightened by the use of cloth tassels as drawer pulls. A contemporary metal lamp, a chinese rice bowl, and two oriental-style frames with prints are placed on the top surface of the chest, leaving it relatively uncluttered and simple.

A folding screen, standing to the side of the oriental chest contains family photographs, bringing additional color into the calm space around it.

97

design idea 98
10-minute tip: Add a bead to the top of a tassel to dress it up.

This large bead and silk-threaded tassel soften the overall look of the front of this cabinet door. The splash of color enhances the painting on the door.

design idea 99
10-minute tip: Tie a tassel onto the key of a locking cabinet.

The simplicity of the Oriental metallic tassel adds a subtle textural embellishment. The furniture piece is the focus, and the tassel is the finishing touch. Keeping the tones similar to the woodgrain adds detail without distracting from the armoire.

design idea 100
10-minute tip: Wire a bracelet onto a plain metal drawer handle.

This beaded handle adds a bit of whimsy as well as an informal element to a piece of furniture, bringing visual delight to the viewer. It takes only a thin piece of wire and a beaded bracelet along with a playful attitude to complete this great look.

99

100

design idea 101
10-minute tip: Tie tiny charms onto tassels for ornamentation.

Tassels come in an infinite variety of styles and materials. They can be handmade or mass produced. Regardless of how they are made, they are always a wonderful accent piece for just about anything. This tassel has small trinkets attached to its fringe and adds charm to the doorknob.

design idea 102
10-minute tip: Attach dried fruit and flowers onto pieces of ribbon for decorating drawers and pulls.

101

These dried orange slices tied onto a piece of ribbon with other small bits of embellishment are particularly festive for the holidays as well as being long lasting. There are a great many items that can be tied together with ribbon or cording to add accent.

design idea 103
10-minute tip: Cut up greeting cards for colorful labels on drawers and files.

Antique wooden filing drawers are a great way to store many useful items. Colorful bits of gift wrap and wallpaper are a whimsical way to label their contents. The contents are handwritten on each label. It feels more personal and "Old World" in this way. A simple heart accent is attached to a ribbon and slipped over a drawer pull.

102

design idea 104
10-minute tip: Fill a small evening bag with sachet and hang on a drawer pull to add scent to a room.

So many times, elegant evening bags and sachets are tossed into a drawer and forgotten. Instead of storing them, hang the evening bag, filled with sachet, on a dresser drawer pull. Every time the drawer is opened, the fragrant scent is released, adding yet another lovely detail.

103

Work areas such as kitchens and offices do not have to be formal and mundane. The heart pull on this cupboard puts a little love into this kitchen when the family chef prepares the meals.

design idea 105
10-minute tip: Attach three different handles onto a cupboard instead of two that match.

Notice how the knobs and handles were used together—very daring and unique. Dare to be different! When decorative elements like these handles and knobs were put on this cupboard, it changed the entire mood in this kitchen.

106

105

design idea 106
10-minute tip: Place a metal cutout behind one of the cupboard knobs.

The addition of the unusual knobs and the metal heart cutout brought these plain doors to life. It is an inexpensive and playful way to address a small space.

The selection of accessories makes as much a statement as the knobs and handles on the cupboards. Whether the choice is to decorate with two stacked earthenware bowls containing perfect pears, or colorful trivet tiles accented with a decorative bottle, let it speak of you. This being the canvas—it is entirely up to the individual on how much it says.

107

design idea 107
10-minute tip: Use different colored knobs on cupboard doors.

These little jewels add color and interest to a white wall full of cupboards. The knobs give a focal point to the built-in hutch and tie into the colors in the rest of the kitchen. Different colors are used on each of the knobs, because things do not always need to match.

design idea 108
10-minute tip: Display an assortment of colorful bottles and dishes.

Colorful bottles and glassware are displayed along with a teapot, mugs, and plates. Here again, the items on display do not have be a matching set, their shape and color will unite the entire collection.

108

If one is bored with the way something looks—a shelf or a table—add a little something to spice it up, or take something away to dress it down.

design idea 109
10-minute tip: Use candleholders to elevate items displayed in cabinets.

This teapot needed to sit higher, in order to fill in the blank wall behind it. Two metal candlestands were found, and worked great because they complemented the design in the teapot and cups. Rummage through closets and drawers; oftentimes what you need is within your reach.

110

111

design idea 110
10-minute tip: Use dress pins for napkin holders.

When an item is used unconventionally, such as these ornate dress pins as napkin holders, one is using their creativity. The pins that look so terrific on napkins will look great on a jacket lapel later in the week.

design idea 111
10-minute tip: Place some glassware up and some down in the cupboard instead of all the same direction.

Who says everyday glassware has to be sitting up or down? What about splitting the difference? In this cupboard, the glasses are alternately up and down. Opposites do attract the eye.

Unconventional uses for conventional items leave the impression of creativity and individuality when decorating.

design idea 112
10-minute tip: Use tissue paper in place of more conventional containers.

Tissue is used to accent these freshly picked pieces of fruit. Line a basket or other container with tissue or other type of paper. There are a great many types of paper to work with and the colors are endless.

design idea 113
10-minute tip: Mount old buckets or cans onto walls.

Weathered sap buckets were mounted unevenly onto the wall above a potter's bench. They are painted with a tantalizing combination of colors with several tilted ever so slightly.

The glass containers, grape hyacinths, and oranges arranged on the tabletop are just as intriguing as the tins above them. The casualness of this display is deliberate.

Bobbles, bangles, and beads—what splendid colors and shapes jewelry can have. Perhaps you have a necklace or other piece of jewelry you want to display at all times.

design idea 114
10-minute tip: Drape a necklace on a shelf as an accent.

Attach a bead necklace by entwining and draping it around a metal shelf. Two beaded tassels further embellish the shelf, and three golden pears are placed on top.

design idea 115
10-minute tip: Display jewelry on the outside of a jewelry box.

114

Just because an accent piece such as this Chinese jewelry chest has drawers, doesn't mean that the jewelry has to be hidden inside. Necklaces and bracelets are arranged on top of the chest and over a glass tripod bowl. Miniature shoes and a tile with cranes in flight make a small vignette.

design idea 116
10-minute tip: Use something other than a jewelry box or tree to show off favorite pieces of jewelry.

A vintage soap dish, holding necklaces and bracelets in a variety of styles and colors, complements an ornate silver-plated mirror. What a lovely display for the top of a bedside chest.

115

design idea 117
10-minute tip: Use an old dress form in the place of a tall potted plant.

Scarves and ornate dress pins adorn this old-fashioned dress form in place of clothing. Any jewelry or other item used or worn by women are themes that work well together when it comes to decorating the dress form. Find uses other than the expected for showing off special and unique items.

116

119

An oversized bath towel sitting on a bamboo chair in the guest bath is another way to place ready-to-use items.

A large serving bowl filled with a variety of seashells sits on the floor to one side of the chair, creating an atmosphere of serenity and tranquility.

design idea 120
10-minute tip: Tip a basket or container on its side for an additional storage shelf.

A simple wooden shelf, housing towels within a basket and stacked towels, is only made more thought provoking when the legs to the shelf are actually decorative clay pots. Two unusually shaped bottles and a handthrown clay container are the only other accents in this display of simplicity.

design idea 118
10-minute tip: Use an aged table such as a potting table to hold towels or bedding.

A collection of everyday items, such as soaps and cotton balls in glass containers, and buckets filled with fresh flowers are displayed among the towels on an old potting table, creating an interesting grouping. This display is all about details.

design idea 119
10-minute tip: Use a chair to hold fresh towels in place of a towel rack.

120

Storage is always a challenge when one wants to store the trappings of a hobby or a craft, while still requiring easy access to those items or supplies. Remember that a hobby or craft is an art form and take pleasure in displaying the tools of the craft. Supplies need to be visible and easily accessed when it is time for creative juices to flow.

design idea 121
10-minute tip: Old hutches and cupboards are a creative solution for storing sewing or craft supplies.

This older cabinet is home for sewing supplies such as bobbins of thread, pin cushions, scraps of vintage lace and fabric, and bolts of ribbon. Fabric-covered boxes, glass bottles, and ceramic dishes hold small sewing notions such as buttons and pins. Not only do the sewing supplies find storage in this well-worn cabinet, but they embellish it as well.

design idea 122
10-minute tip: Remove drawers and use as shelves for those hard to store items.

Faux-finished cabinets with the center drawers removed provide storage for an assortment of decorative and handmade papers.

design idea 123
10-minute tip: Old glass showcases or other furniture pieces that are open on top are good storage for wrapping papers.

Additional papers are stored upright in an old glass showcase. These rolls of paper are easily stored where the colors and patterns can be seen at a glance.

122

123

Stacking chairs on chairs, a chair on a side table, pillows in front of pillows, or an oversized mirror on a trunk are great ways to invent a personalized look.

design idea 124
10-minute tip: Stack similar items in graduated sizes.

Stacking chairs on chairs in three graduated sizes is whimsical and somewhat reminiscent of a favorite fairy tale, with a small giftwrapped box placed on the seat of the smallest chair.

125

design idea 125
10-minute tip: Use doll furniture as servers on the countertop or at the table.

This miniature red chair, amidst all the blue, ties the framed print and the fresh roses into the room décor. The chair seat offers an additional surface on which to stack a homemade jar of jelly.

design idea 126
10-minute tip: Stack books by color, topic, and size as a decorative element in the study or living room.

The mirror commands dramatic attention while the trunk provides the mirror with a sturdy foundation on which to rest. The velvet pillows stacked on the chair lend harmony to the striped wallpaper, and a small footstool serves as another surface on which to place these favored books.

124

127

It is not often that one would think to use shoes as a decorative element or accent. It is more common to think that shoes should be put away out of sight. Baby's first pair of shoes may be bronzed or porcelain-covered to preserve them and the memories they evoke.

design idea 127
10-minute tip: Display shoes as if they are an artform.

The simple tilt of the shoe is no accident, but a coy statement of the time period that these shoes represent as well as an artful presentation. Chairs are also oftentimes works of art and this chair is no exception. It is used as a backdrop for this wonderful pair of nineteenth-century shoes and sets an atmosphere of nostalgia. Light flooding through a window covered by sheer white curtains and potted ivy are subtle touches.

128

129

design idea 128
10-minute tip: This white-on-white ensemble is dramatic, especially with the small touches of color in the fruit and flowers.

The white vase with peonies takes the spotlight in this grouping. The green leaves point down, drawing the eye towards the tiny hatbox with a young girl's shoe. The eye is drawn, next, to the perfectly shaped pears in a white bowl. This is a restful and soul-pleasing display of accessories.

design idea 129
10-minute tip: Display sports equipment as a decorative element and in a way that suggests they are ready for use.

A woven-wicker rocker, sitting on a built-in porch tilts back slightly from the weight of old leather ice skates. The casual feeling created here makes one feel welcome as well as inferring the opportunity to indulge when a frozen pond beckons all skaters.

10-minute tip: Use children's toys, antique or new, as a decorating accent.

A pine hutch filled with lace, antique tablecloths, quilts, and a small tea set defines a room for vintage children's toys—or an adult who loves such things. A stocking made from collected pieces of fabric, lace, and ribbon, filled with a handmade teddy bear, adorns the hutch doors the entire year. A larger teddy

bear, dressed in an heirloom christening dress, waits expectantly for a special visitor.

design idea 131
10-minute tip: Display quilts on the wall and framed artwork on a bed or sofa.

This bed has unusual "guests" when two framed needlepoints are placed with the pillows. The idea of a quilt on the wall and frames on the bed is a delight. Hatboxes are stacked to the right of a small round pedestal table, with a miniature lamp and vintage telephone placed upon it. Nothing ordinary in this guest room!

130

133

design idea 134
10-minute tip: Tie delicate neck scarves around metal objects such as this metal mirror.

The hard metal edges of this unique and free-standing mirror is softened by a neck scarf with a tassel. The lavender bottle and casually placed scarf, sitting on the tabletop, also ease the angles.

design idea 132
10-minute tip: Look for an original use for items other than what they were designed for.

This Chinese serving cabinet is placed in the bathroom to be used for cotton balls, swabs, and other toiletries. A statue of Quin Yin stands where the sewing bobbins would ordinarily be placed. The orchid adds balance and color to the overall setting.

design idea 133
10-minute tip: Create a shelf within a shelf to display miniature objects so they can be more easily seen.

A small shelf within a shelf provides an additional place and allows for a more intimate look at the miniatures, the tagged and labeled bottle collection, and the embellished frames and albums.

134

Chapter 6

Mother Nature

One cannot resist the beauty of nature, whether it is in planting a garden and tending it, or bringing the outdoors inside through flowers—fresh or dried. Bringing nature into the home may also include accents in a sun room, or a planter that is versatile enough to be used either indoors or outdoors.

design idea 135
10-minute tip: Use a chair or bench as a plant stand.

Lilacs and hydrangeas get the seat of honor on this bamboo-backed chair. The color and diversity of real flowers are endless and an effective way to adorn any space.

design idea 136
10-minute tip: Bring outdoor planters indoors and put them to use as a centerpiece.

An array of foliage and flowers is combined in an old and aged clay pot that can be brought inside and used as a centerpiece.

design idea 137
10-minute tip: Embellish plain flowerpots with artificial fruit.

This dried lavender topiary is sitting pretty on a stack of hatboxes. Wire-edged ribbon, artificial fruit, and other dried botanicals were hot-glued onto the terra-cotta flowerpot and topiary.

136

137

design idea 148
10-minute tip: Bring a porch swing indoors during winter months.

Items meant to be outside in our gardens, like this porch swing, are often too difficult to give up. Swinging inside this garden room, one feels that soothing sway of "summer" all year.

design idea 149
10-minute tip: Setup a hammock that stays indoors all year long.

Many types of outdoor furniture from our gardens can end up inside. However, one does not often think of a hammock in that way. The easy flow of the hammock in a sparsely decorated room affords one an opportunity to relax and ponder.

148

149

design idea 150
10-minute tip: Stand up old shutters and hang garden tools from them.

Outdoor shutters capture the seed packets and tools for my garden. Nestled in among the shrubs along a brick wall, it seems natural for them to be there. The garden tools are hung on hooks and the seed packets are tucked in between the louvered slats. In a kitchen, the shutters might contain tips from your mother's "Recipes for Living" journal, or in the laundry room, they could hold hangers.

design idea 151
10-minute tip: Stack graduated sizes of metal buckets with an assortment of florals and fruit inside each one.

Three sizes of rustic floral cans are stacked one atop another, making a striking arrangement when dressed up with limes, golden yarrow, and purple statis. This arrangement also could be featured sitting on the floor by a door, or as a centerpiece in a garden setting.

151

design idea 152

10-minute tip: Fill flowerpots with pinecones, evergreen boughs, and florals for a holiday arrangement.

Bringing the outdoors inside keeps me more grounded during the winter. These terra-cotta flowerpots were gold-leafed, then filled with an assortment of florals and botanicals. Scattered around the base are fresh roses that look very festive.

design idea 153

10-minute tip: Place potted evergreens into buckets.

Two pine trees have a dressed-down look in these oversized buckets and either inside or out, they look at home. They also could be decorated with old metal ornaments, sparkle glitter, or anything else that would not be ruined by outdoor inclement weather.

design idea 154

10-minute tip: Sprinkle potpourri around the base of dried and silk floral arrangements.

This preserved spiral evergreen stands tall in a Renaissance-period container. Tucked among the branches are velvet pansies, with potpourri encircling the base of the tree. It smells wonderful and the flowers never fade.

153

154

125

155

design idea 155
10-minute tip: Use a carved pumpkin as a Fall center-piece or kitchen decoration.

Celebrate autumn in the kitchen with a carved pumpkin. A fish motif is the theme, rather than a frightening or whimsical face. Walnuts and hazelnuts are scattered at the base of the pumpkin, adding to the fall theme. The bottled whole carrots speak of the harvest and bring color and additional texture to the grouping. Several types and shapes of bottles and dried flowers tie it all together.

design idea 156
10-minute tip: Stack lighted jack-o'-lanterns vertically and horizontally.

This grouping of carved pumpkins has been stacked in two rows. Different facial expressions were carved into each one, giving them their own unique and distinct personality.

design idea 157
10-minute tip: Place a carved and lit pumpkin in an entryway with a gas lantern.

Jack-o'-lanterns are seen decorating porches everywhere, so why not indoors? This scary faced pumpkin lantern sits beside a gas lantern, adding light and mood to the entryway.

156

157

158

Chapter 7

Lighting

Decorating with lighting encompasses more than selecting a decorative light fixture. It is the placement of fixtures, embellishment of fixtures, or the use of electric light and candlelight.

design idea 158
10-minute tip: Place a handkerchief or small shawl over the top of a lamp shade.

An exquisite sheer shawl, trimmed with lace and crystal beads, is draped over a white linen shade and dresses up a table lamp that has few complex design elements. The lamp is further accented by a bromeliad sitting next to it on the end table. It lights up a space next to the sofa and becomes the perfect reading lamp when curling up with a good book.

design idea 159
10-minute tip: Hang ornaments on a chandelier to embellish a plain lamp fixture.

These three metal cones, adorned with beads and lace trim, look like posie holders. They not only add a twist to a rather plain iron light fixture, but also complement the windowpane design behind it.

159

Small lamps are often used to light small areas and to enhance a particular mood. There is a large variety of lamps, plain and embellished, which can be purchased to accent a specific area or simply because of their sculptural and art qualities.

design idea 160
10-minute tip: Use jewelry, ribbon, and silk florals to accent a lamp that has few embellishments.

This tiny lamp is placed in front of a sheer curtain and delicately lights up the space around it. A string of small pearls is twined over the ombré ribbon wrapped around the stem and base of the lamp. The ribbon complements the silver-beaded lamp shade. Silk pansies adorn the beaded areas of the shade.

160

161

design idea 161
10-minute tip: Display a single "special" accent on a tabletop or shelf by itself.

This "young lady" brass lamp is a work of art in, and of itself. A desk or table may call for a distinctive design or clever light source. This lamp does not require a number of other accent pieces, since it is meant to be admired for itself. It stands on a small round table and is accented only by the framed artwork hung on the wall.

design idea 162
10-minute tip: Place a metal drawer pull or finial on top of a lamp shade for decoration.

The beaded-fringe lamp shade was discovered at a rummage sale and the challenge was to find a lamp base that would complement the shade. A plain and inexpensive lamp base was found, then wrapped with multiple layers of sheer ribbon and accented with leaves. The lamp shade was topped with a metal drawer pull as the final accent.

163

design idea 163
10-minute tip: Place a table lamp in front of a mirror to reflect the lamplight.

The small lamp brightens the walkway in this entry where it sits low to the ground. The lamp also highlights the decorative accessories beside it, as well as reflecting light off the mirror behind it. Notice the small vases that have been placed on the floor on either side of the table.

design idea 164
10-minute tip: Place a standing lamp next to a small table to highlight the accessories placed upon it.

This hand-painted lamp shade rests on a copper and pewter lamp stand, which in turn accents the silver-leafed table and vases on it. The pattern in the lamp shade has a leaf design that complements the other florals in the room. The lamp highlights a beautiful table and the floral placed upon it.

design idea 165
10-minute tip: Tack a beaded necklace or choker around a lamp shade.

A lamp fixture and silk shade trimmed with beads points upward instead of down, and the warm glow of light softens the ambiance in this room. By turning the fixture upward, it does not interfere with the potted orchid sitting directly below it.

164

165

166

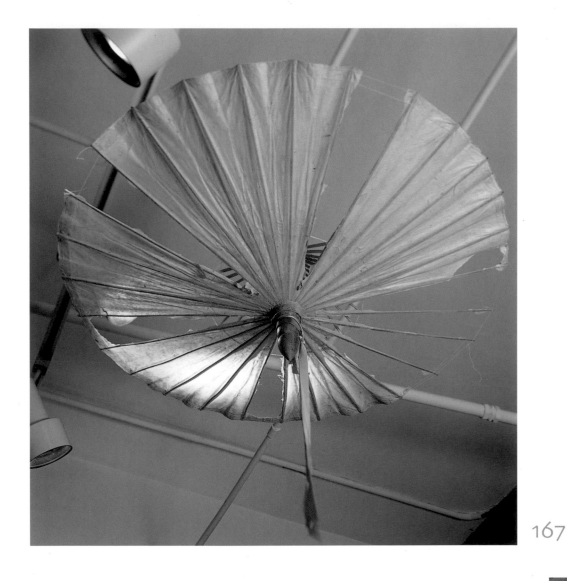

167

design idea 167
10-minute tip: Age a paper parasol by tearing pieces from the ribs.

One parasol was torn to suggest a weathered atmosphere and to create interest.

design idea 168
10-minute tip: Hang paper parasols from the ceiling.

By mixing color, patterns, and a few torn parasols, a mosaic effect was fashioned among the rafters that is unexpected, but well worth noticing. The light filtering through the tissue illuminates the parasols' designs and is an added bonus that is also cost effective.

design idea 166
10-minute tip: Tack and drape a wearable or a length of fabric to the ceiling.

Parasols filter light and draw the eye away from the unsightly pipes and track lighting in this room. Between the collection of paper parasols, a Sari is attached to the ceiling and draped. Each parasol is hung with a colorful ribbon.

168

10-minute tip: Place a lamp on a low surface and allow the light to radiate upward.

Not all light has to come from above eye level. This tall table lamp is perfect for a low Chinese-style side table. The gentle spiral of the silk shade is a dramatic design element that looks great, whether it is lit or not. The message that comes from the combination of the lamp, the chinese side table, and a chair that has been covered with various patterns and textures of fabric is that furnishings and accessories need not come from the same time period or style.

design idea 170
10-minute tip: Drape strings of beads around a chandelier.

Lamp shades can change a chandelier at once. Formal silk shades may add drama, whereas these beaded shades suit this gypsy chandelier. Strings of beads were draped and looped around the lamp fixture. The brass chandelier was purchased from a local thrift store.

169

10-minute tip: Mix and match candlesticks on the buffet or dining table.

Three different styles of crystal candlesticks reflect the light from the nearby window. The candle-light reflects against the windowpane, creating a play of natural light and firelight. The candle-

sticks allow the sunlight to filter through and refract off the cut glass.

design idea 172
10-minute tip: Display candle-sticks on a bar tray with other bar accessories.

Here, the candlelight and can-dlesticks sitting on a bar tray are duplicated by a mirror hung on the wall. This is a crystal and glass combination resembling ice touched by the warmth of candlelight and reflected back into the room. The glass vase of fresh florals also adds a touch of warmth and life.

171

design idea 173
10-minute tip: Float candles and blossoms in a shallow serving dish.

Floating candles, combined with sprigs of fresh flowers, are an inviting sight in any bathroom or entry. The combination of fire and water creates a contrast that is pleasing to the senses. A clear bowl was used in this arrangement, but any type of container, ceramic, metal, or clay, could be used, depending upon the environment that one desires to create.

design idea 174
10-minute tip: Create an arrangement with candlesticks and florals.

The single white rose floating in a crystal cup and the cala lillies nestled in among these lighted candlesticks bring together a cooling effect from the flowers to the fire element.

design idea 175
10-minute tip: Make floating candleholders from drinking glasses.

Colored sea glass and fresh herbs in water, topped with a floating candle, can light up any kitchen counter with a refreshing natural look. The color combinations brighten the glass and can be customized to suit any kitchen or dining area.

174

175

10-minute tip: Place tiki torches into a floral arrangement.

A sense of opulence is created
for indoors or out, when
Hawaiian florals are combined
with tiki torches. The concept
of placing candles among
flowers may not be so new
and unique, except that the
torches stand three feet tall.
Try something new and daring
when decorating with lighting.

176